PEOPLE WE KNOW

SNIGDHA TIBREWAL

to everyone who has ever been hurt,

may your heart remain breakable but never by the same hand twice.

Contents

Contents

Somewhere within your loving look I sense,
    Without the least intention to deceive,
    Without suspicion, without evidence,
Somewhere within your heart the heart to leave.

VIKRAM SETH

Acknowledgements

"A dream you dream alone is only a dream. A dream you dream together is reality."

— Yoko Ono

My first debt is to my parents, who provided me with everything I could ever possibly need including the encouragement to try my hand at whatever I wanted. Know that this wouldn't be possible without you.

Thank you to my sister, who has always been the first to read everything I have ever written, even the books I didn't end up writing. You will always be my role model and I owe all the best things in my life to you. I love you, Jojo.

To my best friends, thank you for being my beta readers. There's nobody else I would've rather shared my book with first. To the reader, if this book makes you feel something, thank them or blame them at your own discretion.

To my wonderful friends Aprajita and Kabir, who have done all the illustrations for this book. Thank you for taking a chance on me. You guys were my dream team.

To the most lovable weirdo Gia, who is my grammar coach both in real life and for this book. Thank you. You know all my commas would have been missing without you.

To everyone who wonders if I'm writing about them. I am. And lastly to my 8-year-old self, thank you for picking up a pen and paper.

You'll find someone in here.
Someone you know.
Because these people, they are your mothers
And fathers and brothers and sisters and friends.
These people
Are ***you***.

Déjà Vu

"Already seen"

1. Amaira

At 2 she walked,
At 3 she talked,
Her parent's pride she really was
Her future lay in front of her;
Meticulously planned
Since the day she was born

18 was for college,
23 for a job,
25 would see a marriage,
27, and a boy was to be born

But oh, lord
She got pregnant at 19!
And if that wasn't enough shame for her parents
Later in life, she became the D-word
You know, we say it in hushed tones:
It's "Divorcee".
And that was the end of the world for her parents
Because neighbor aunty was talking about it
Over chai so nonchalantly:
"There go the parents of the girl pregnant at 19!"
But why can't it be-

'There go the parents of the single mother who did all that and still got a degree?'

So they went to the doctor's
Because her skin had started to hang from her bones, you see
She wasn't eating well-
At all actually.

Because whatever society put on her parents,
They put it on her.
The doctors read books,
But I read people
And I have a diagnosis:
She does have a disease
Because she was fed every day
10 milligrams of 'what will people say?'

2. Yohan

Peace:
Six feet under.
Earth:
In earth, I'm covered.
Mahogany:
I can smell it off me.
Coffin:
From the giver of life,
A tree.
Wood dead;
Tree alive.
And me?
I'm soaked in irony.

Afraid I would end this way:
Pain,
Silence,
Grief.
Remembered today,
And then I wither away.
I was so scared,
But now I wonder why

Closing my eyes,
It was pain at first;
But then the peace was high.

What is left for me to see?
My home?
Welcome to the 21st-century machine.
Humans:
Humane no more.
People:
Friends or foe?
It's better to die than live and breathe
This air
In today's world,
It may be fake just like
You and me.

Earth:
The constant.
Us?
Variables.
Mere humans in a game of snakes and ladders,
Backstabbing and pushing to reach
The very end.
But that's the trap, my friend,

Your prize awaits at the bend.

Death:

Open arms

An unflinching smile.

You smile too,

But at your foolish mind.

Mere humans like me so afraid of dying,

But little do they know,

No matter how far you go,

You can never leave it behind.

It lurks in the shadow,

To grab its next prey.

We all go to sleep but there is always one,

Who never wakes.

3. Kabir

My face is bashed;
Cuts and bruises.
My eye is smashed;
And blood it oozes.
My father's belt;
It's black with blue.
And it hits my face,
Hard, not loose.
I stole the lipstick from my mother.
The skirt I tried on,
Was pink with purple.
But now red:
Blood red is my color.

All my friends wanted to be superman,
But I was more of a wonder woman fan.
I was a disgrace,
Because I wanted to change.
But to be me was all I wanted
And that didn't make me sick or wrong or crazy:
It made me human.
I was blamed,
For my 'condition'

But what would they know?
They were just 21st-century robots,
With a narrow-minded mission.

4. Kiah

I found an age-old bottle of pickle,
Behind jars of cinnamon, paprika,
And vanilla truffles.
It reeked of nostalgia,
Just as it did of oil.
It reeked of
Sunday mornings at home;
Breakfasts and second servings
I never managed to deny.
But that was for a fraction of a second
After that, all I got,
Was a whiff of turmoil.

Ma and Baba were grounded people;
And all I wanted was to fly.
And when they couldn't fly with me,
I left them behind.
They, I decided were too deep in this oil,
Knee deep in tradition, roots and the people of their kind
This was just as the waiter arrived,
'Ma'am, here is your fat-free gluten-free mocha latte chai'

It had been 20 years:

And still, I wondered,
Had I done right?
Was cutting my roots from under me,
The only way to fly?
Because nothing had ever compared to
Ma and Baba's
Parantha, pickle, and homemade chai.

5. Sara

They were slow dancing on the marble floor:
The click of her heels,
The tap of his shoes,
Somewhat rhythmic,
As they waltzed to the tune.

She had known him forever, it seemed:
Since they were little kids,
Running under hues of orange,
On the beach.

But suddenly his hands moved down,
From her back
To the curves to which she was bound.
And this made her nervous,
Sweaty all at once:
Uneasy, nauseous, uncomfortable.

But this thought she left forlorn,
Because she had known him for so long,
And trust is measured by the time that's gone.
But his hand was moving down slow,
To places she didn't want him to go.

So she took it and placed it back on her waist,
And said 'No, don't.'

And all he did was smile:
That sly smile.
He said,'but surely that's not a no:
Inside it has a hidden yes.
Not something that can't be brought out,
With my persuasion at its best.
Surely that's not a no,
Because you've known me for so long.
Surely that's not a no,
Because your answer is yes,
You just want to be teased first, correct?'
And she was appalled:
Had she known him for too long?
Had the time put a veil on what he really was?
She took a step back,
But he pulled her in.
So she said,
'When I say no,I mean no.
There's no hidden yes.
I say what I want:
Full stop, there's nothing else.'

'But no one says no to me!'
His ego was hurt.

And that's the problem you see:
He had never been told no,
Since he was small.
A girl belonged to a boy:
That's what he was taught.
So now he got what he wanted,
Either by consent or by force.

But she was lucky:
So she ran as fast as she could.
And all she could think was,
'What happened to consent?
A yes is a yes:
And a no a yes as well.'
And that mentality is being taught to little kids
With every passing breath.

Later he got through to another girl,
Reported, arrested, sitting in the lock-up:
Beaten up by sticks so long,
Screaming, "No! please don't!"

And all I can wonder is:
Now that word is supposed to mean something to us?
Is now a 'no' enough?

6. Avi

'I wish you were dead.'
That's the last thing she said.
And I think about it all the time:
All the time I have left anyway.

As I lay here bleeding,
Closer to the sky than to the ground:
Closer to where there is peace,
Than where is sound.

Why should I have said sorry?
It's not like the fault was mine.
Anyway I have tomorrow,
And the rest of my life.
But that's the trouble,
We think we have time.

Time to breathe,
And live,
Exist, and be,
Time to grow,
And cherish,
And make families.

To say "Sorry"s,
And "Thank you"s,
"I miss you"s and "Please".
Time to live and love,
And laugh as long as we need,
But that's not the-

7. Shaveri

There was a little house
On the hill.
Lived in it a princess
And her prince.
When they opened their curtains,
Everyone would see.
When they danced in the rain,
So did everyone in their vicinity.

There was a little house
On the hill.
Lived in it a princess,
And her prince.
She wanted to be someone,
Do something for herself.
He wanted her in the kitchen,
And then straight to bed.
So he'd twist her hand,
Smile with a gleam:
Throw away,
The hope of her dreams.
When they opened their curtains,
No one met her eyes.

When she cried in the rain,
No one was there,
Up to miles.

There was a little house
On the hill.
The princess was gone,
But the prince still lived.
But don't drop a tear,
Because this isn't about him:
It's about the princess.
In our memories,
That's where she still lives.
Every day she died a little;
Death was no punishment.
It was the living,
The breathing,
That she resented.

Déjà Senti

"Already felt"

8. Noor

I can't breathe
With anxiety pumping in my veins
And uncertainty causing chest strains.

Tears welling up in my eyes,
Questions running in my mind,
Of whom to become
And what to do.
But I don't even know about tomorrow
Who am I to speak of ten years through?

And if I don't do good,
I'm expected to do better.
And if I do good,
I'm expected to do it forever.
And on top of that,
You have to get enough sleep,
And look great,
And have a social life entirely.

So once in a while,
When it all gets to my godforsaken head,
My chest is blocked,

My throat is locked
And I can't speak or breathe or feel,
But it's supposed to be okay:
"Shush!"
They say;
Because we all can't breathe I guess.
But I have trouble figuring out,
I do;
How we can't breathe,
Is not the problem.
But the solution,
To make it feel like it's any less.

And I want to tell you,
I do;
But I look at you,
And all that comes out is "Hi!"
And so when the system gets the very best of me
Like it does every once in a while
You'll regret, not asking why.

9. Inaya

I'm sick;
Stuck with a disease,
Called "Try and make every boy you meet fall in love with you, please".

And it's fine for the most part,
Until it's not
Until I get caught,
Up in it all.
And then I fall,
Into the abyss of questions.

When my heart flutters,
I'm filled with tension:
Is this real?
Or a side effect, a symptom, so to say,
Fluttering away,
Do I really like him?
Or is it just my sickness on a whim?
Brim:
I'm filled to the brim.
But I don't let it pour out,
I've had days to practice.

And so the "Maybe"s get lost with the "No"s,
Wasted potential on the floor.
And I sit once again with my disease,
Cursing its existence,
My loss, its gain.
Cursing it,
for blurring my sane and insane.

10. Ayana

She can't walk down the street
Without two men howling,
Three whistling,
And one eve-teasing.

Can't travel by train
Without being stared at in full,
Or getting 'accidentally touched',
When the brakes get pulled

She's scared sometimes to take a walk in the park,
Because she's told,
You're asking for it,
When she wears her favorite tank top

Or because the guys who stare at her,
When she gets off at her stop,
Just maybe the ones to rape her,
And leave her somewhere in the dark

So she's taught herself,
To cover up to the top,
And 'be safe',

Whenever she walks

So when she's on the train
It's always the women's box,
And traveling in a cab,
Means keeping a friend's number on top

Looking at every man in her life through the eyes of suspicion,
Because to survive as her,
Is now a lifelong mission.

It doesn't matter
If she's someone's daughter or sister,
She shouldn't be raped,
Because she's a human.

And she's scared,
Because she wants to make it through life
Without getting ripped or raped,
Touched without her consent
So what do we say?
And we, not our masks
What she's saying,
Is it too much to ask?

11. Geet

Hopeless romantic,
A boy perfect for her soul
They had something
Something that could go till the very end,
But somehow she knew,
That this was not what was meant

Hopeless romantic,
Boy with a reputation
Cliché stood still,
As she fell without knowing
Nobody thought she was going;
Going to fall into his arms,
Is what she believed
From the outside, it was picture perfect,
But who knew what was going underneath?

She fell,
He didn't catch,
So she lay on the floor all alone.

She was angry, disappointed
Tired and broken,

Sick, scared
The sadness she's soaking;
In a world full of people, yet she's choking
Put her hand out,
But there's no one to hold it.

She finds him;
In every sad song,
In everything done wrong,
In every sunset,
In her every breath,
In every damn quote,
In every sinking boat.
And in all things dark;
In a black crayon,
Black ink,
In a black hole
Until she realized she had two arms of her own.

Hopeless romantic,
Romantic no more
A believer of facts,
Love existing? That's a joke
Or maybe it did,
She just didn't know.

Whatever she was trying to find out there,

She had to learn,
Had been in here all along
That,
That is what the foolish heart of hers,
Had yet to know.

12. Kavya

She's the queen
Of the cursed land,
With tall towers,
And luscious lawns.

She's got every jewel you can name,
And courtiers to play games,
She's got her gentlewoman
To help her dress,
And servants at her beck and call
For when she makes a mess,
And subjects that agree with everything she says,
No obstacles in the path that lays.

You'll see her everywhere
With everyone,
But never anywhere
With someone in particular.

Everybody watches the queen,
But nobody sees her
Sees that she's so alone,
That she's got

Friends and family,
And subjects and a home,
But she's so terribly alone

And they say after everything's said and done,
That's the price you pay for being,
The chosen one

But I see the way,
She sees her friend
Watches her uninhibited laughter,
The way she questions,,
Watches her be free of
Chains that hold her back,
The way everyone sees her
The real her,
And not her mask

But she's afraid to tear off her own,
Because her mask is one thing she's had all along
"What if"
"What if", she wonders,
"They'll only love what they see
And not the one,
I don't let myself be?"
"What if
I'll never be more than a good girl?

Because I'll never be her."

And she laughs
Because she tries,
And tries and tries,
But she's never her,
Or her or her,
Or anyone but herself
And is it a curse or a boon,
Is yet to show itself.

13. Anokhi

I wish he loved me,
Like he loves her,
That someday I was more than
Her friend sitting in a corner

Because I see you,
But you don't see me
I'm here, you're here
But only she exists in our reality

A planet stuck in her orbit,
Addicted to her like a fiend
I try to pull away,
Until I realize I'm just a part of her,
But she's all of me

I'm the best friend, the encouragement,
The hand to hold on to when you're scared
The one who's clapping,
But never the one who's up on stage

And it's fine,
On most days I make my peace;

Until it's something,
That only comes around once
A shooting star never repeats,
But more like star-crossed lovers that never meet

So I wish that he loved me,
Like he loves her
But no matter what I do,
Love will always be given,
And not earned.
So once in a blue moon,
In a moment of weakness,
I wish
That he wanted
Kavya's friend instead:
That one day,
I'll be the poem
And not the poet.

14. Itihaas

"Born prematurely",
Said the doctor with a certain sadness in his eyes,
"A memory
You shall live of her",
He told my parents,
She's just too thin, too fragile

That hospital room was to see the last of me,
A full stop to the sentence of
My life;
But it ended up being a semicolon,
To my surprise
And that's where we take a deep dive

Growing up I'd see these compelling models
Thin and fair,
Everything they did with a certain flair
Their skin is so clear,
Nothing out of place,
Not even a single hair

And my idea of beauty,
Was slowly confined

Trapped in a box,
Made of limits and lines

Girls that I met yesterday,
I wouldn't recognize today
For they had changed the way they looked,
Because that's what it took

And boys starving for abs,
They may not want but need
From what we've heard,
Well-built strapping lads
Is just what the world needs

But it wasn't till a fine day that it hit me,
That I had been conditioned to see
A specific picture of beauty:
Fair, with high cheekbones and thick lips,
Thinner waist but thicker hips
Or perhaps it was:
Tall but not too tall,
Muscles but not too many,
Too many boxes to check,
And very little time, if any

And only one question was running circles in my mind
Then where does even-

The line
The limit,
The so-called standard of beauty reside?

It's a fine line of beauty,
That we're here walking
Too thick and you're fat,
Too thin and you're starving
Too much makeup and you're hideous,
For the so-called society
No make up,
And you're mundane
Boring, not exciting
This line of beauty is itself,
Contradicting,
Confusing, shifting
Like a labyrinth,
It's moving.

The bigger the wrinkles on your face,
The finer it is
More experience you've gained,
But a waistline the smaller the better they say.
Too left,
Too right,
You can't shift in this game
Beauty is now a line,

Tightrope walkers, we stand
Trained and tame

But wasn't beauty supposed
To be any color, shape, or size
That we picked,
That you and I liked?

Because beauty is not only in the perfect glass vase
It's in the broken pieces;
That we don't embrace
It's not borders and limits,
It's a ground completely unimpeded,
We look different but we're still alike;
Because the line,
The limit,
The bar,
The standard of beauty
Is to be the person that you are
Not the one you look like.

Déjà Visité

"Already visited"

15. Maya

Beads of sweat glided
Right across her face
To her chin,
Until she wiped it off
With a scented wipe,
In an instant

It smelled of wild grass,
And jasmine
Picked specifically for her,
From some small insignificant village across the world

It was hot and humid,
And her throat was dry
So she decided to sip on,
Some sparkling water with ice

As the glistening sweat,
Soon turned into air
Outside her window, she gazed,
Saw some village children running in a
Summery haze

Into her fur slippers,
She slipped her feet
To write a paper,
She opened up
One of her many screens
And so she wrote,
'Poverty and how it's being cured'

But, was it?
Because those children weren't running,
To and fro
They were running away,
But how could she have heard;
The AC was too loud anyway.

16. Ishaan

How is it that the world is so loud,
Yet my mind only craves peace?
How is it that I smile by the day,
But the night only brings tears?

How is it that I'm surrounded by people,
Yet I'm alone?
How is it that one minute I'm up there,
And another I'm down?

Is it because peace amidst the chaos is what I want to find,
Because when the raindrops fall,
The night also cries.
Is it because masks are not people, just mere variables,
Because when I'm up, the down is not far from where I'm to be found,
I'm just upside down.

17. Aisha

A little girl with pigtails,
With dreams and hopes,
That one day she would make
More friends than she could count,
Achievements that would surmount,
Anything and everything:
That someday,
She would be somewhere,
From where they couldn't bring her down

Tick-tock,
Tick-tock,
Life went on like a clock,
Before she knew
She was yee big,
With her hair pulled back in a ponytail,
All slick

You could say she was new to life
The bubble had just been broken,
It was nothing like the storybooks had told her,
But she didn't want to judge a book by its cover,
Divulging a little perhaps would help her

So tick-tock,
Tick-tock,
Life went on like a clock
She was now thin and tall,
The hair tie in her hair,
Tighter than it had ever been before

What she saw was that life was grey,
You could be black or white:
But blue, yellow, green?
Don't even mention their name

In real life,
There weren't any see-saws,
Swings or funny slides,
All she could hear was:
Left-right,
Left-right,
That monotonous marching
That went on for days,
Of whom you ask?
Of us, the greys

But she had read all those quotes on the net,
They said to be happy, not sad
So she kept waiting for the

Good after the bad,
The good after the bad,
The good after the-
She couldn't even remember anymore,
She had been waiting for too long

When the boy broke her heart,
She said, "Okay, I'll move on",
When the friend stabbed her in the back,
She said, "It was okay,
I guess everyone gets conned"
But when she started feeling lonely,
That's when worry had filled her cup

A few days ago,
I saw her on the ledge,
Of the building's terrace
Her hair was neatly folded in a bun so tight,
That any moment the vein in her temple would pop out,
Like it was done
That's all I gave her,
A minute of my time,
Funny you ask why
I had to get home right?
I had worries of my own,
This that and life.

The next day,
Bold letters and underlined,
The headline caught my eye,
The little girl with the pigtails had died.
I didn't understand then,
But I do now

She died many deaths,
Before her final breath,
What I saw was an empty shell:
No soul.
The little girl with the pigtails?
She died long ago.

18. Dev

Nobody is born,
A cheat or a liar
But you don't know,
What goes on behind closed doors

You don't know the pain or the anguish,
Or the poison in my mind;
Or all the crying at night:
Alone,
That I hide

All you know is,
When the cameraman pulls out his camera;
I put on a show,
And pull out my smile

But you fail to realize that,
My smile is a satire,
And that's the moment,
I become a liar

And why do you fail to know?
Because you are the characters in my satirical show.

19. Aryan

My superhero,
It's been six days since you died,
Six since our last fight,
And six since I hurt you out of spite

I can't remember a time,
When I didn't wish for you to die,
When we weren't at each other's throats,
With daggers up to our nose

And yet I stood behind the trees tonight,
As they buried you deep inside,
If only to pretend,
That a part of you was still here;
Still alive

And don't be mistaken,
I still hate you,
Enough to set my bones alight
But the only other who understood that hate,
Were you,
And you're out of sight

The stories said,
We were too different
Of a coin,
We were on opposite sides
You the hero
Flying around,
Saving the days
I the enemy,
Only ever the Harbinger of disgrace.

But they failed to mention,
In the footnotes,
Of the story of our lives
That head means nothing without tails,
That they are one coin,
Never separate

And I prided myself,
On being alone all my life,
But I never was, truly:
Until tonight.
Because you were the day to my night,
You haunted my dreams,
And I tainted your daylight
Because I fought;
But I fought with you,
Even if not by your side

And I hated;
But I hated you,
And you did just the same all your life
Because I don't know when,
But you became a passenger,
On the train of my life
A thorn in my side;
Unwanted,
But still there the same alright

How could have I been so blind?
To not see that we were on the same train boarded,
From platforms on opposite sides
That if I hurt you I would hurt just the same
If you were gone,
I would too be a memory
In a grave:
That without a superhero
A villain is nothing but a name.

On a single ticket,
I travel alone,
For the first time in days,
Wishing you stayed,
If only to argue another day,
This is far from a love letter,
But only you and I know,

There's a thin line between love and hate
So I settle down in my seat,
With only the ghost of you
To keep me company
And in the quiet of the night,
When everything ceases to be,
I miss your bickering;
Our chaotic peace.

Yours truly,
The villain that you'll never see

20. Ojas

I close my eyes
And I find myself there,
Breathing borrowed air
The bustling of the people and the cars
And the city,
Calms me
Home to the dreamers that never sleep,
Calling my name,
Just like it did when I was 12,
Just the same

And my body knows it's home,
Because it's not always where you're born,
Sometimes that's just bricks and windows and a wall:
A house, not a home;
A difference learned long ago

So what if I run north?
Not from but to
Where I was always supposed to be
Making my way back really,
And just as that crosses my mind,
I run out of time,

At Times Square
And my chest constricts from the
Lack of air
I open my eyes;
A little part of me dies
Because maybe I know I'll never be there
It'll exist only in folklore,
And I'll look for it,
Forevermore.

“What’s past is prologue.”

- Shakespeare, The Tempest

About The Author

Snigdha Tibrewal is a 16-year-old student currently studying at Sardar Patel Vidyalaya. Born and raised in New Delhi, she has been an avid reader since a young age. Writing since the age of 8, she believes that poetry is just one's pain finding a medium of expression. You can find her painting, dancing, or listening to music when she's not writing.

Her first collection of poems *People We Know* is an anthology of life experiences among other things filled with themes of heartbreak, consent, domestic violence, and death, a collection she would've liked to come across herself at this age. The idea for *'People We Know'* was conceived upon her realization that the strongest relationships in her life were based on people finding a piece of themselves in each other.

The book aims to make the reader feel a little less alone in the experiences they've had and remind them of the people they have come across in life.

You can find her presence at:

www.instagram.com/where_the_wild_words_grow